All for our Rightful King

Traquair's Jacobite Story
1688 - 1842

Catherine Maxwell Stuart & Margaret Fox

Traquair
Scotland's most southerly Jacobite stronghold

CONTENTS
ಐ

Foreword--4

Setting the Scene---5

Traquair's Jacobites--7

The Royal Jacobites---8

Birth of the Jacobite Movement------------------------9

An Unhappy Marriage of Nations----------------------14

The 1715 Jacobite Rising-----------------------------------19

Escape from the Tower of London---------------------25

Dispatches from 'O'er the Water'-----------------------31

Life in Exile---36

The 1745 Jacobite Rising----------------------------------42

Aftermath of the '45--48

Last Vestiges of the Jacobite Dream------------------52

Acknowledgements---56

FOREWORD

The history of Traquair is inextricably linked to the Jacobites in part due to the iconic landmark that stands at the top of our entrance - the Bear Gates.

When the Earl of Traquair closed the gates in 1745 following the visit of Prince Charles Edward Stuart and promised they would not be opened until a Stuart king was crowned once more, little did he know that they would remain shut for over 250 years, and would stand as a poignant reminder of one of the most famous lost causes in Scotland's history.

Yet the Stuarts of Traquair were Jacobites long before the 1745 uprising and the 4th Earl of Traquair was imprisoned for his Jacobite sympathies as early as 1692. Their loyalty to the cause derived from their faith as Roman Catholics and their strong links and service to the Stuart monarchy that went back to the earliest years of the dynasty.

The family's survival through this troubled period was remarkable and perhaps due to some astute political manoeuvres, although they were regularly fined and imprisoned for their beliefs. It is also fascinating to look at the role the women of Traquair played, not only in supporting their husbands but also, in the case of Lady Nithsdale, planning her husband's escape from the Tower of London.

As a mark of their loyalty, the family treasured a fine collection of Jacobite glass, portraits and miniatures as well as other Jacobite memorabilia that can still be seen in the house today.

In 2015, the 300th anniversary of the Jacobite Uprising of 1715, we mounted an exhibition at Traquair that pulled together all the strands of the family's Jacobite connections and their stories throughout this period, as well as the repercussions for them following the final defeat at the Battle of Culloden.

This book tells that story through original documents and letters held in the archives at Traquair that reveal the family's association with this revolutionary cause.

Catherine Maxwell Stuart
21st Lady of Traquair

Setting the Scene
Traquair's Loyalty to the Stuart Monarchy

☙

Traquair's Jacobite story follows the momentous events in British history sparked by the Glorious Revolution of 1688, interwoven with the personal stories of the Stuarts of Traquair. Their unwavering loyalty to the Stuart monarchy forced into exile in that year shaped the family's destiny for a century, and has had a lasting impact on it down to the present.

This publication allows the inhabitants of Traquair House and their close relatives, the Maxwells of Nithsdale, to narrate their allegiance to the Jacobite cause in their own words, set in the broader political and religious context. It is a poignant tale of a family fighting for its beliefs.

The family's loyalty to the Stuart monarchy dates from 18 May 1491 when the Earl of Buchan, uncle to James III of Scotland, gifted the "barony of Tractware" to his son, James Stewart, who became 1st Laird of Traquair - marking the start of the ancestral line which continues to the present day with Catherine Maxwell Stuart, 21st Laird (Lady) of Traquair. The 1st Laird died with King James IV at the Battle of Flodden in 1513.

For almost a hundred years the Stuarts of Traquair faithfully served the monarchy, with John, William and James, the three younger grandsons of the 1st Laird, holding positions of responsibility in the Royal Household. John, the 4th Laird, was knighted by Mary Queen of Scots in 1565 and appointed Captain of the Queen's Bodyguard. William, 5th Laird, served as Gentleman of King James VI's Bedchamber, and James, 6th Laird, was Lieutenant in the King's Guard under his brother, Sir John.

Moving into the 17th century, John, the 7th Laird of Traquair, was granted an earldom by King Charles I during his Coronation visit to Scotland in 1633, and appointed Lord High Treasurer of Scotland in 1636. John was, in effect, the king's right-hand man in Scotland, having to implement his unpopular measures like the introduction in 1637 of the Anglican Book of Common Prayer into the Church of Scotland. Impeached by the Scottish Parliament in 1641, the Earl of Traquair nevertheless remained loyal to the king.

Setting the Scene

Taking part in the English Civil War on the Royalist side against Oliver Cromwell's 'Roundheads', the earl was captured at the Battle of Preston in 1648 and imprisoned in Warwick Castle until 1652 – by which time his family had suffered financially and the Stuart monarchy had been replaced by the Commonwealth, with Cromwell about to be declared Lord Protector.

The execution of King Charles I on 30 January 1649 marked the end of the service of the Stuarts of Traquair to a reigning monarch, but their loyalty to the Stuart monarchy was to continue…

> **When Charles's younger son, King James VII of Scotland (II of England and Ireland), was forced into exile in 1688 it is hardly surprising that they would rally to the cause of restoring him to the throne.**

ෆ

In 'All for our Rightful King' the exiled King James VII of Scotland and II of England and Ireland is designated King James VII. His son, Prince James Francis Edward Stuart, is referred to as King James VIII from his father's death in 1701.

The printed title pages in Chapters 1 and 2 are from pamphlets purchased by the 4th Earl of Traquair and bound into volumes preserved in the Traquair House Library.

Traquair's Jacobites
ෆ

Charles Stuart, 4th Earl of Traquair (1659 - 1741) and his wife, Lady Mary Maxwell (1671 – 1759)

William Maxwell, 5th Earl of Nithsdale (1676 - 1744) and his wife, Lady Winifred Herbert (1672 – 1749)

Charles Stuart, 5th Earl of Traquair (1697 - 1764) and his wife, Theresa Conyers (d. 1778)

Setting the Scene

The Royal Jacobites

King James VII of Scotland, II of England & Ireland (1633 – 1701) second surviving son of King Charles I and younger brother of King Charles II. Three years into his reign he was forced into exile as his Catholicism was unacceptable to the Protestant majority in the English Parliament.

Prince James Francis Edward Stuart (1688 – 1766) whose birth led to the Glorious Revolution. Following the death of his father, King James VII, in 1701 King Louis XIV of France recognised him as King James VIII of Scotland and King James III of England and Ireland. Otherwise known as the 'Old Pretender'.

Prince Charles Edward Stuart (1720 – 1788) elder son of King James VIII. He led the 1745 Jacobite Rising in an attempt to place his father on the throne of Great Britain and thereby restore the Stuart monarchy exiled to France in 1688. Otherwise known as the 'Young Pretender', 'Bonnie Prince Charlie' and the 'Young Chevalier'.

Prince Henry Benedict Stuart (1725 – 1807) younger son of King James VIII. On his brother's death in 1788 Henry publicly claimed the throne of England, Scotland and Ireland, with remaining Jacobites recognising him as King Henry IX. However, the papacy did not support his claim and he made no attempt to instigate a further Jacobite rising. He became Cardinal Duke of York.

Birth of the Jacobite Movement
1688 – 1692

☙

"Our ancient crown's fa'en i' the dust"

(from James Hogg's 'Jacobite Relics')

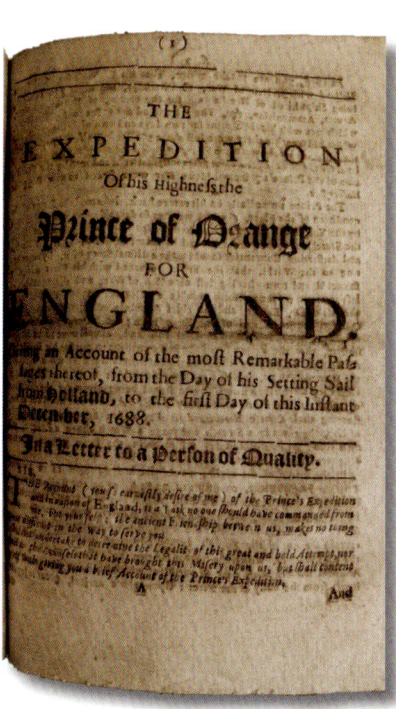

Prince James Francis Edward Stuart, son and heir of King James VII and his Roman Catholic second wife, Queen Mary Beatrice (Mary of Modena), was born on 10 June 1688. His birth led to the 'Glorious' (or 'Bloodless') Revolution only a few months later, had ramifications well into the following century and left a lasting legacy on the Scottish psyche.

Following his accession in 1685, King James's policies of toleration to religious minorities had been giving cause for concern in political circles, and his own Catholicism was deeply disturbing to many. Until the birth of his son, James's successor to the throne would have been his elder daughter, Mary, a Protestant married to his nephew, the Protestant William of Orange. A Catholic son and heir was unthinkable to a majority of English Parliamentarians who invited William to invade England and remove James from the throne.

William landed at Torbay, Devon, on 5 November 1688, and news of the Protestant invasion spread quickly to Scotland. As the only Catholic stronghold in the Borders, Traquair immediately found itself a target:

Anno 1688 Upon the News of the Prince of Orange his Landing in England, the Suffering and Contending Party of Presbyterians in Scotland from a General Meeting Sent Certain of their Number, under the Command of Daniel Ker of Kersland, to the Lord Traquairs house to Search for Popish Trinkets.

All which were Solemnly burnt at the Cross of Peebles

Inventory of 'Popish Trinkets' forcibly removed from Traquair House, December 1688

"A Pot full of holy oyl"

"Mary and the Babe in a Case, most curiously wrought with a kind of Pearle"

"A large Crucifix of brass"

The Stuarts of Traquair had renounced Catholicism at the Scottish Reformation in 1560 and John Stuart, the 2nd Earl, had served as an elder in the local Presbyterian Kirk. He had, however, married two Catholic wives, and returned to "*the true religion*" on his deathbed in 1666. His widow, Lady Anne Seton, had brought up

Birth of the Jacobite Movement

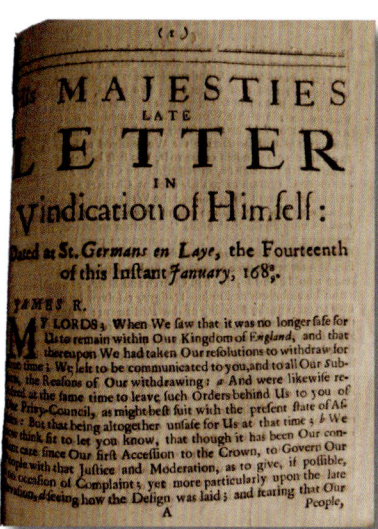

their children as Catholics despite the attempts of the Kirk and the Privy Council of Scotland to force them to relinquish their faith.

King James was forced into exile in France on 23 December 1688 and made his way to the Chateau of St. Germain-en-Laye lying just outside Paris. It was gifted to him as his new residence by his ally, King Louis XIV, who had moved his Court to the Palace of Versailles a few years earlier. The exile of James and his entourage to France marked the start of the Jacobite movement (after 'Jacobus', Latin for James).

It seemed probable that Charles Stuart, the young 4th Earl of Traquair, would come to the attention of the authorities now on the lookout for likely Jacobite sympathisers. Only three days after the king left England, he received a letter from his cousin, the Duke of Queensberry, who did not share his allegiance to the Catholic king, advising him not to do anything hasty:

…In the Mean tyme It's fitt ye live as abstract as possible, without giving ground of Noice, or Intertaining any body in your familie that may Alarum, or give raise for Tumult…

Duke of Queensberry to Charles, 4th Earl of Traquair
26 December 1688

Birth of the Jacobite Movement

1689 witnessed important constitutional change. In February William and Mary were proclaimed King William III of England and Ireland (II of Scotland) and Queen Mary II of England, Scotland and Ireland.

On 11 April the Scottish Parliament declared James to have forfeited the Scottish throne. And in December the Bill of Rights, the legislative framework of the Glorious Revolution, stipulating that in future *'no popish prince'* could *'inherit, possess, or enjoy the crown'*, was passed by the English Parliament. James attempted to regain his crown through war in Ireland, but was defeated by William at the Battle of the Boyne on 1 July 1690, an event which was to have lasting consequences.

William and Mary
joint monarchs from 1689

ଔ

As a staunch Roman Catholic it was probably inevitable that the Earl of Traquair would become involved in Jacobite activities before too long. He was briefly imprisoned in the summer of 1692, three months after the Massacre of Glencoe when thirty eight members of the MacDonald clan had been killed for not having pledged their allegiance to William and Mary by the end of 1691.

The Duke of Queensberry again gave his cousin advice:

... soe in my humble opinion It's fitt your lop [Lordship] give Exact obedience to the Counsells letter, without saying or doing anything to give your Enimies Advantage, or occasion Noice And when yow have bein In prison a few dayes I'm verry hopefull that upon my Ladies Application And Reneu'd Attestations of physitians that your Liberty may be procur'd.

To add to his distress, Charles was suffering ill-health.

The young Charles Stuart
4th Earl of Traquair
1659-1741

Duke of Queensberry to 4th Earl of Traquair 12 May 1692

The duke observed that he was: *"**Abundantly Convinc'd of the hard Measure yow gett, Bot to Strugle now is to noe purpose bot to doe harme… I'm Confident this Alarum will over one way or other in few dayes**"*.

Queensberry wrote to Charles again on hearing of his release from prison the following month:

This is to Acknouledge the honour of your Lops [Lordship's] of 11th Current, by which I am glad to find yow at freedom, And Doe hope In short tym, ye shall Recover your health…

Duke of Queensberry to 4th Earl of Traquair, 11 June 1692

But there was further imprisonment to come…

An Unhappy Marriage of Nations
1702 – 1709

"We were bought and sold for English gold
Sic a parcel o' rogues in a nation"

(Attr. Robert Burns)

Anne, the Protestant younger daughter of King James VII, became queen in 1702 following William's death without an heir. By this time it seemed likely that Anne would die childless, having had numerous unsuccessful pregnancies, and her only surviving son, William, having died in 1700. The English Parliament had already taken measures to ensure a Protestant succession to the thrones of England and Ireland after her death with the passing of the Act of Settlement in 1701. This named the Electress Sophia of Hanover, a granddaughter of King James VI (I of England and Ireland), as Anne's successor.

Queen Anne
b. 1665 - d. 1714

Scotland and England had shared a monarch since the Union of the Crowns in 1603 when King James VI of Scotland inherited the English throne on the death of Queen Elizabeth I. The Kingdom of Scotland and the Kingdom of England had, however, remained distinct, each with their own parliament. The English Act of Settlement did not meet with unanimous approval in the Scottish Parliament, as evidenced by the printing of this anonymous work, *'Speeches by a Member of the Parliament which began at Edinburgh the 6th of May 1703'*.

It concluded: " *'tis my Opinion, That the House come to a Resolution, That after the Decease of her Majesty, heirs of her Body failing, we will separate our Crown from that of England"*.

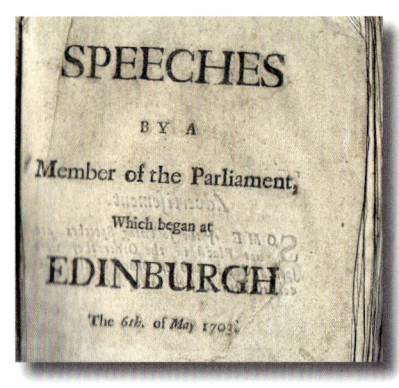

With the matter of Queen Anne's successor not entirely resolved and with the fallout from Scotland's disastrous attempt to

An Unhappy Marriage of Nations

establish a trading colony on the Isthmus of Panama in the Gulf of Darien in the late 1690s, influential sections of both Scottish and English society, each with their own political agenda, came to support the concept of a single kingdom, crown and parliament. The topic of a full union of the two nations was about to be hotly debated on both sides of the border.

The years between 1702 and 1706 saw the appearance of many pamphlets on this highly divisive subject. The Earl of Traquair amassed quite a collection in order to gain an understanding of the issues involved, buying publications advocating union as well as those opposing it, and those giving a more balanced perspective.

In September 1706 he paid a bill which included these items:
A letter against the union
[Daniel] Defoe's two bookes of the union
Hodge's or Redpath's new considerations on the union
The Lord Haversham's considerations on the union

Account of Alexander Strachan with 4th Earl of Traquair, 20 September 1706

An Unhappy Marriage of Nations

Opposition in both countries was overcome, and the Treaty of Union was agreed on 22 July 1706. Following ratification of the treaty, the Act of Union with Scotland and the Act of Union with England came into effect on 1 May 1707 - and the United Kingdom of Great Britain *"for ever after"* was created.

Henceforth Westminster in London would be the home of the unified parliament and a Protestant succession to the unified throne would be assured.

ೞ

Less than a year later the uneasy equilibrium in Great Britain was rocked when an attempt was made by James Francis Edward Stuart to invade Britain and restore the exiled Catholic Stuart monarchy. The French king, Louis XIV, had recognised him as the rightful king of England, Scotland and Ireland following the death of his father, King James VII, in 1701. Early in 1708 Louis offered James a number of troops to bring across from France to support him in his endeavour. They were conveyed in a large fleet towards Scotland where they hoped to receive backing from the vast majority of Scots who resented the Union.

With the young and hopeful King James VIII on board, the ships headed for the Firth of Forth to land near Scotland's capital, Edinburgh. The British government had, however, received intelligence of their progress north, and they were intercepted by a Royal Navy fleet under the command of Admiral Byng at the mouth of the firth. Thwarted in their attempt to land, James and his French supporters were forced to retreat back to France.

ೞ

By April 1708 the Earl of Traquair, a known Jacobite, found himself again imprisoned in Edinburgh Castle, but he seems to have suffered very little hardship on this occasion. He wrote to his wife, Mary, ***"my Dearest hart"***, back at Traquair:

"all Papists...shall be excluded from and for ever incapable to Inherit Possess or Enjoy the Imperial Crown of Great Britain and [its] Dominions"

(from Treaty of Union)

King James VIII
b. 1688 – d. 1766

> I long extreamly my Dearest hart to see you so if your health can allow I would have you take the opportunity of your Mothers Coatch to come here I thank God I am in perfit health and hath not been so well their severall years as I have been since I cam here wherfor I beg as you love me not to be discouraged for what els shall happen to me the bearer will informe you fully what is ordered about all the prisoners give my humble duty to your mother and my Blissing to the Bairns I am my Dearest Life inholy yours
>
> Traquair
>
> Castle of Edinburgh
> 22. Aprile 1708

"my Dearest hart…"

4th Earl of Traquair to his wife, Edinburgh Castle, 22 April 1708

I am in perfit health and hath not been so well their severall years as I have been since I cam here", and a short while later: ***"The castle air gives me a good stomach. We have very good company here and liveth very pleasantly The only thing that troubleth me is the want of you.***

Mary, although several months' pregnant, decided to join her husband in his captivity, leaving **"the Bairns"** in the care of her mother, the Dowager Countess of Nithsdale. On hearing the news of her son-in-law's imprisonment she had travelled from her home at Terregles in Dumfriesshire to be with her daughter and grandchildren at Traquair. On 12 May William, one of the elder boys, wrote poignantly to his mother: ***"Wee will all be in pain till wee see your Ladyship and my Lord come safly home, which I pray god may be soon"***. However, there was a delay in them returning home – upon release, the earl had to attend to urgent business affairs down in London, and Mary chose to travel with him.

Disheartened by the abortive Jacobite invasion in 1708, the Earl of Traquair continued to suffer for his beliefs close to home. There was continuing disapproval from the Kirk for his Catholicism. In 1709 he received this letter from the Presbytery of Peebles:

My Lord. The presbytery of peebles having this day had a letter from the Commission of the General Assembly making mention of several Acts of parliament, and Acts of the General Assembly of this National Church anent Papists, injoining the Judicatories of this Church to do what is incumbent upon them for the reclaming of them from their errours, and the having of their Children educated and trained up in the knowledge of protestant principles, and finding it their indispensible duty to do every thing that's proper for them for the good of your Noble Family, have appointed two of their Brethren... to wait upon your Lordship at your house upon the eight day of September next to converse with your Lordship anent the ends above specified...

It was recorded in the next set of minutes that the earl *"was not at home"* on the appointed day.

"*the having of their Children educated and trained up in the knowledge of protestant principles*"

Charles Stuart
4th Earl of Traquair
1659 - 1741

The 1715 Jacobite Rising
1714 - 1716

"It was a' for our Rightfu' King"
(Robert Burns)

King George I
Great-grandson of
King James VI/I
b. 1660 d. 1727

John Erskine
Earl of Mar
1675-1732

Queen Anne died on 1 August 1714 without an heir, as expected, and the Act of Settlement, passed by the English Parliament in 1701, came into effect. The throne was offered to George, Elector of Hanover, son of the Electress Sophia of Hanover whose death had also just been announced. The accession of George I established the Hanoverian dynasty in Great Britain.

Considerable pressure had been put on James VIII to convert to Protestantism but he had firmly resisted this effort. His renunciation of Catholicism might well have safeguarded the House of Stuart, but it was not to be.

In 1714 there remained a significant amount of loyalty to the exiled Stuarts throughout Great Britain and Ireland, and particularly in Scotland. This loyalty crossed both political and religious divides. The Union of 1707 had not been a success either, with measures in the House of Lords to dismantle it in 1713 only narrowly failing.

By mid-1715 there was growing resentment building up against the new Hanoverian monarchy. In Scotland the leader who emerged was John Erskine, Earl of Mar. He had served in Queen Anne's administration but, as a Tory, had switched to the Jacobite side when he was overlooked for office by King George who favoured the Whig party. This earned him the nickname 'Bobbin' John'.

The 1715 Jacobite Rising

James VIII had been corresponding with the Earl of Mar, and in the summer of 1715 James called on him to raise the Highland clans. Mar left London for Scotland, convening clan leaders and fellow Jacobite supporters to "*a grand hunting-match*" at Braemar on 27 August. The 4th Earl of Traquair is thought to have attended this gathering. The city of Perth was captured on 14 September without opposition, with the Earl of Mar setting up camp there to await further developments.

October 1715 saw much Jacobite activity further south. There was a strong contingent from Northumberland which included two prominent Catholics from families which staunchly supported the exiled Stuarts - James Radcliffe, 3rd Earl of Derwentwater, and William Widdrington, 4th Baron Widdrington, who had both spent much of their youth in the exiled Stuart court at St. Germain-en-Laye. The Northumbrians under General Thomas Forster joined forces with troops assembled from across the south of Scotland under Viscount Kenmure, and they were joined by a body of Mar's troops at Kelso in the Borders.

William Maxwell
5th Earl of Nithsdale
1676 - 1744

☙

William Maxwell, 5th Earl of Nithsdale, and brother of Mary, 4th Countess of Traquair, joined this united force although he had no natural inclination to take up the sword. In 1699 he had visited St. Germain where he had met his future wife, Lady Winifred Herbert, daughter of the 2nd Marquess of Powis in Wales. Winifred had lived in the court there, her father having served as King James VII's Lord High Chamberlain and her mother as governess to the young Prince James Francis Edward. However, William had been back in Scotland, at the Maxwell family home at Terregles in Dumfriesshire, long enough to recognise where his duty lay. He had the support of his brother-in-law, Charles, who, fearful of a third spell of imprisonment, chose not to take up arms. He remained at Traquair in order to protect his estates.

Lady Winifred Herbert
5th Countess of Nithsdale
1672 - 1749

Jacobite troops laying down their arms in Preston 14 November 1715

'View of the Rebels, as they were brought Pinion'd to London'

The troops continued south into England en route for London, and by the time they reached Preston in Lancashire on 9 November 1715 their numbers had grown to around 4,000. However, Hanoverian troops, despatched from Manchester under General Charles Wills, engaged them in skirmishes in the streets, gained the upper hand and forced the Jacobite surrender on 14 November. The previous day the Earl of Mar's forces had clashed with Hanoverian troops under the Duke of Argyll at the Battle of Sheriffmuir. This had proved inconclusive in spite of Mar's superior numbers.

The 1715 Jacobite Rising was virtually over before King James VIII had set foot on Scottish soil. He finally arrived on 22 December, landing at Peterhead, to be met with the dismal news. Realising that the cause was all but lost, and accompanied by the Earl of Mar, he boarded a ship for France from Montrose on 5 February 1716. Mar was to be given a role in James's court in exile and would never return to Scotland.

Vignette from a contemporary print depicting 'The Six Lords Pleading at Westminster Hall'

The trial of William, 5th Earl of Nithsdale, and the other five most prominent Jacobites who had been captured at the Battle of Preston and conveyed to the Tower of London, was taking place at the same time as King James was making his way back to France. They had all been charged with high treason.

Sentence was pronounced by the Lord High Steward on 9 February 1716:

James Earl of Derwentwater, William Lord Widdrington, William Earl of Nithisdale, Robert Earl of Carnwath, William Viscount Kenmure, William Lord Nairn;

You stand impeached, by the Commons of Great Britain in Parliament assembled, of High Treason, in traiterously imaging and compassing the Death of His Most Sacred Majesty; and in conspiring, for that End, to levy a bloody and destructive War against His Majesty, in order to depose and murder Him; and in levying War accordingly, and proclaiming a Pretender to His Crown to be King of these Realms.

... that you, and every of you, return to the Prison of The Tower, from whence you came; from thence you must be drawn to the Place of Execution; when you come there, you must be hanged by the Neck, but not till you be dead, for you must be cut down alive; then your Bowels must be taken out, and burnt before your Faces; then your Heads must be severed from your Bodies, and your Bodies divided each into Four Quarters; and these must be at the King's Disposal.

And God Almighty be merciful to your Souls!

"your Heads must be severed from your Bodies, and your Bodies divided each into Four Quarters"

Rev. John Scott, who was with William attending to his spiritual welfare, wrote to Mary, Countess of Traquair, waiting anxiously to hear news of her brother:

In my last I gave Your Ladyship an account of the fatal sentence pronounced against the six Lords who had pleaded guilty. Their submitting themselves to King George's Generals att Preston to avoid the effusion of Christian blood, their acknowledging themselves guilty, and their imploring mercy has availed them nothing. The warrant for their execution was signed on last saturday, and the day appointed for them to dy is next friday. My tears make me stopp here.... I wish I could stopp or att least mitigate your Ladyships! ... my dear Lord has receiv'd this dreadfull Sentence with an Angelicall resignation to the holy Will of Almighty God, in whom he hopes to find a Mercifull Redeemer...

William himself wrote a final poignant letter to Traquair:

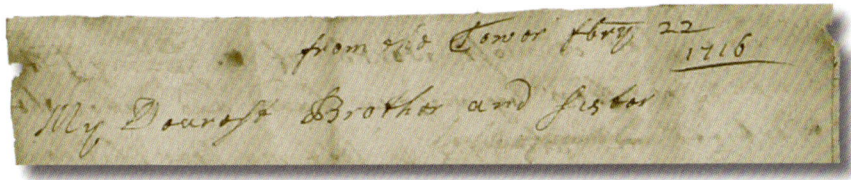

from the Tower fbry [February] 22 1716
My Dearest Brother and Sister

I most willingly make use of some of the most precious moments of my life to give you the last assurance of my tendernes towards your persons, and off my gratitude for your manifold favours, and espesialy for your generosity towards me in these my hard sircumstances, in which you have shewed yoursels true and cordiall friends...

The 1715 Jacobite Rising

William went on to speak of his wife, Winifred, clearly aware of her unsuccessful attempt to secure a last-minute reprieve for him:

Everybody admires her, everybody applaudes her, and extolles her for the proofs she has given me of her love. So I beg of you, dearest brother and sister, that whatever love and affection you bear to me, you would transfer it unto her as most worthy of it...

... as to myself... I am entirely resigned to His most holly will, and humbly adore his Providence. I look upon the time He has graciously been pleased to allow me to expiate my past offences as the surest pledge of His love towards me, and of my future happiness...

William Maxwell, 5th Earl of Nithsdale, remained forthright about his Jacobite loyalties to the end, asserting in his Dying Speech:

... I declare that I drew my sword meerly out of the motive of Justice and piety to assert the undoubted and Hereditary Right of that Prince whom I then believed and still believes to be my only Leige Lord and Lawful Sovereig[n] James the 8th of Scotland, and third of England.

Dying speech of William Maxwell, 5th Earl of Nithsdale

Escape from the Tower of London 1716

On hearing the news of her husband's capture at Preston and his removal to the Tower of London, Winifred, Lady Nithsdale, had been distraught. She hurriedly attended to urgent affairs, locked up Terregles, left her daughter, Anne, with her uncle and aunt at Traquair and headed for England:

I rode to Newcastle, and from thence took the stage to York. When I arrived there the snow was so deep that the stage could not set out for London. The season was so severe and the roads so extremely bad, that the post itself was stopped. However, I took horses and rode to London, though the snow was generally above the horse's girths, and arrived safe without any accident.

With the day of William's execution fast approaching, Winifred wrote to her sister-in-law on 18 February 1716, expressing her desperation:

Tho I am very unfit Deare Sister to write in ye condition I am in, w[hi]ch Mrs G gave you an account of, & dare not repeat ye melancholy occasion, I have done all I can since, & on munday last I found a way to deliver a petition of my L[or]d's to The K[ing], w[ha]t effect it will have I know not, but I am sure I have left nothing undone that was in my power, & this night am going in to him, where if I am not permitted to stay in the night time, shall take a chamber hard by, & goe in to him every morning & stay all day, for till there is some alteration more in his circumstances nothing more can be done, but for feare I should be confin'd not to goe out if there be any thing can be done hereafter, am resolved to ly out if they doe not promis to lett me out w[he]n I please, but whether I am to lye out or in shall take

"I have left nothing undone that was in my power"

Escape from the Tower of London

**Winifred, Lady Nithsdale, to her *"Deare Sister"* Mary, 4th Countess of Traquair
18 February 1716**

care he shall not be imposed on as hitherto he has been, being forced to trust to their buying every thing he wanted for diet or other necessarys…

The Nithsdales' predicament was already having a severe financial impact on their relatives at Traquair. Winifred, with a degree of shame, continued:

…I cannot tell what excuse to make for my Lord's taking up another Hundred pounds upon your Lord's credit, but I knew nothing of it till it was done, for he has been already so generous

Lady Mary Maxwell
4th Countess of Traquair
1671 - 1759

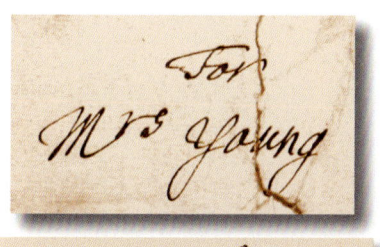

that I am quite out of countenance about it, but I am sure nothing but absolute necessity could have obliged him to it, so I hope he will excuse it, I am sure he nor I can never sufficiently acknowlege ye favours we have received from you may God be your reward & ye prayers of the afflicted shall never be wanting for your prosperity & hapiness both in this world & ye next...

By this time Jacobite supporters had assumed 'noms de guerre', literally, names of war. The Earl and Countess of Traquair were Mr and Mrs Young; William and Winifred, 5th Earl and Countess of Nithsdale, were Mr and Mrs Joanes.

Winifred had just become aware that a last minute pardon was being considered for some of the six lords - but seemingly not for her husband, whose crime was compounded by his being *"A Roman Catholic upon the frontiers of Scotland... a man whose family had always signalized itself by its loyalty to the royal house of Stuart, and who was the only support of the Catholics against the inveteracy of the Whigs, who were very numerous in that part of Scotland"*.

On the eve of the execution, Winifred resorted to a final desperate measure - orchestrating a daring plan for William's escape from the Tower. Some time later she recounted every detail of this to her sister, Lady Lucy Herbert, bringing it vividly to life in a thrilling narrative:

...such an old story now, that I have almost forgot it... so hazardous an enterprise, wich I fully intended not to go about till the very last, foreseeing all the difficultys wich could not be surmonted without a particular protection of almighty God but relyd it would not be refused me...

Before launching into details of the escape Winifred recalled her frantic effort to deliver her petition to King George:

Escape from the Tower of London

I threw myself at his feet, and told him, in French, that I was the unfortunate Countess of Nithsdale, that he might not pretend to be ignorant of my person. But perceiving that he wanted to go off, without receiving my petition, I caught hold of the skirts of his coat, that he might stop and hear me. He endeavoured to escape out of my hands, but I kept such strong hold that he dragged me from the middle of the room to the door of the drawing-room. At last one of the blue ribbands, who attended his Majesty, took me round the waist, whilst another wrested the coat out of my hands. The petition, which I had endeavoured to trust into his pocket, fell down in the scuffle, and I almost fainted through grief and disappointment. One of the gentlemen-in-waiting took the petition...

Escape from the Tower of London

Then she went on to relive the dramatic events of the subterfuge:

... I went partly down stairs to meet Mrs Mills, who had the precaution to hold her handkerchief to her face, as is natural for a woman to do, when she is going to take her last farewell of a friend on the eve of his execution. I had, indeed, desired her to do so, that my lord might go out in the same manner. Her eyebrows were rather inclined to be sandy, and my lord's were very dark and very thick; however, I had prepared some paint of the colour of hers to disguise his with; I also brought an artificial head-dress of the same coloured hair as hers, and painted his face with white and his cheeks with rouge, to hide his long beard which he had not time to shave. All this provision I had before left in the Tower. The poor guards, whom my slight liberty the day before had endeared me to, let me go quietly out with my company, and were not so strictly on the watch as they usually had been, and the more so, as they were persuaded, from what I had told them the day before, that the prisoners would obtain their pardon. I made Mrs Mills take off her own hood and put on that which I had brought for her; I then took her by the hand and led her out of my lord's chamber, and in passing through the next room, in which were several people, with all concern imaginable...

The Nithsdale Escape, no.19 in a series of 25 'Famous Escapes' on cards issued by Carreras of London with packs of Turf cigarettes in 1926

When I had almost finished dressing my lord in all petticoats except one, I perceived it was growing dark, and was afraid that the light of the candles might betray us, so I resolved to set off. I went out leading him by the hand, whilst he held his handkerchief to his eyes. I spoke to him in the most piteous and afflicted tone of voice…

… I had before engaged Mr Mills to be in readiness before the Tower, to conduct him to some place of safety, in case we succeeded. He looked upon the affair as so very improbable to succeed, that his astonishment when he saw us, threw him into such a consternation that he was almost out of himself;

… When the news was brought to the king, he flew into an excessive passion, and said he was betrayed, for it could not have been done without a confederacy. He instantly dispatched two persons to the Tower, to see that the other prisoners were well secured, lest they should follow the example. Some threw the blame on me, some upon another.

"the wind could not have served better if his passengers had been flying for their lives"

… Mr Mills came and conducted my lord to the Venetian Ambassador's. We did not communicate the affair to his Excellency, but one of his servants concealed him in his own room till Wednesday, on which day the Ambassador's coach and six was to go down to Dover to meet his brother.

… My lord put on a livery, and went down in the retinue, without the least suspicion, to Dover; where Mr Michel (which was the name of the Ambassador's servant) hired a small vessel, and immediately set sail for Calais. The passage was so remarkably short that the Captain threw out this reflection, that the wind could not have served better if his passengers had been flying for their lives, little thinking it to be really the case.

... A lady informed me, that the king was extremely incensed at the news. That he had issued orders to have me arrested... and that I had given him more trouble and anxiety that any other woman in Europe.

William, Earl of Nithsdale, may well have been reprieved – of "The Six Lords Pleading at Westminster Hall", all sentenced to death for high treason, only Viscount Kenmure and the Earl of Derwentwater were executed. They were beheaded on Tower Hill on 24 February 1716.

Vignette from a contemporary print depicting the beheading of the Earl of Derwentwater and Viscount Kenmure

Dispatches from 'o'er the Water'
1716 - 1718

☙

Charles, Lord Linton
(later 5th Earl of Traquair)
1697 - 1764

Charles, Lord Linton, and the Honourable John Stuart, the two eldest sons of the 4th Earl and Countess of Traquair, had been studying at the Scots College in Paris when the 1715 Jacobite Rising was underway in Britain. They had been kept informed of developments by their mother, Mary.

Charles had written to his mother with a mixture of sadness and relief on 1 February 1716, making reference to *"that affair of Preston"* where the Jacobite forces had been forced to surrender the previous November:

...I am heartily sorry to hear that so many of my good friends and acquaintances have had the misfortune to be engaged in that affair of Preston, & particularly for my Unckle, but at the same time I cou'd have no greater comfort than to be assured that Mr Young [his father, the Earl of Traquair] *was not there...*

Charles, Lord Linton, to his mother, Mary, 1 February 1716

Soon, Charles was able to give her an update on the fate of her brother, William, after his escape from the Tower of London and his clandestine crossing of the Channel to France.

Towards the end of March, Mary received this letter from Charles, with some exciting news:

Dear Mother
Some few days ago I had the satisfaction to receive your's of the eight of Feb: and was extreamly glad to find that my Father yourself & all the rest of the family are in perfect good health, but at the same time was heartily sorry to hear of the dismal condition of our Countrey, occasioned by civil broils & the last ill winter which you say was so very violent in your parts, as indeed it was not otherwise with us. One of the cheifest dutys in my opinion, that a Son owes to his mother, is to comfort her in her afflictions so far as he can, and as I easeily perceived from your last letter how much you was afflicted at the sad state of our Countrey, as it is but natural for every well wisher of it so I think my duty obliges me to give you all the comfort I can, and I am persuaded I can give you no greater just now than to tell you that my Unckle after haveing been despair'd of by all is now perfectly recover'd, he came to town yesterday & stays at present in the same lodgeing with us, he doth not design to stay long here, but has a mind to go some place elsewhere more wholesome to breath in for fear he should relapse into his late sickness...

"my Unckle .... stays at present in the same lodgeing with us"

William was still with his two nephews a month later. At the end of one of Charles's letters home he felt obliged to add a short note to his brother-in-law at Traquair:

My Dear ~~Lord~~ *Brother*
I doe not question but both my sister and you longs to hear from me, and I hope you will not attribut my so long silence to any neglect, or want of sence for your uncomon affection towards me, of which you have on all occasions given me mor then sufficient proofs. I assure you no man can be mor sensible, then I am, for your goodnes nor mor desirus to make you a sutable return.

The Honourable John Stuart
(later 6th Earl of Traquair)
1699 - 1779

William, 5th Earl of Nithsdale, to Charles, 4th Earl of Traquair
24 April 1716

Charles edited this message, replacing William's more formal **"Lord"** with **"Brother"** to emphasise to his father the importance of family ties, hoping that he would continue to support his brother-in-law now facing an uncertain future.

After recovering his health, William frequently visited Queen Mary Beatrice, the widow of King James VII, at St. Germain-en-Laye. By 1716, Mary was still living there with only a few of the old remaining courtiers. In 1712 she had suffered two devastating losses. Her daughter, Louisa Maria Teresa, died of smallpox, and her son, King James VIII, was forced out of France during a tense political situation in Europe occasioned by the War of Spanish Succession - with King Louis XIV no longer recognising him as rightful King of England, Scotland and Ireland, having done so since the death of James's father in 1701.

Old Château at St. Germain-en-Laye

With his young followers, James had headed for the Duchy of Lorraine to the east of France to take stock of his situation and work out his next move.

Early in May 1716 Charles told his mother at Traquair about William's visit to St. Germain when the queen (known in Jacobite circles as Mrs Arther) gave William money to enable him to join her son James who was now at Avignon, a papal enclave in south-eastern France. There was also a touching snippet about James's kindness to William:

He went frequently to see Mrs Arther who was extreamly kind to him & furnished him with money what hasten'd his going away was an invitation of Mrs Arther's Son to him in very obligeing termes, he showed me the letter which was endeed full of kind expressions amongst the rest there is one that I can not omitt setting down here to witt, As long, saith he, as I have a loafe of bread in the world assure yourself you shall allways have a share of it...

Charles, Lord Linton, to his mother, Mary 6 May 1716

However, in the same letter, there was news that the Earl and Countess of Traquair must have been dreading:

...I as soon as My Unckle arrived, reckoning that he wou'd be somewhat low in his pocket, offer'd him any little thing that I cou'd command, not doubting but that my Father & you wou'd allow it, he said that he did not stand in need of any then, however before he went away he asked of me two hundred livers which I immediately gave him.

William made the long journey to Avignon where Pope Clement XI was giving temporary hospitality to James's entourage, into which he had high hopes of being welcomed.

Palais des Papes, Avignon

Two years later, Rev. James Carnegy, the Catholic priest who had been in Paris with Charles and John, gave Mary at Traquair the sad news of the death of Queen Mary Beatrice, recounting her dying words to her son "*to persevere in his profession what ever should happen*" and her undying belief that one day the Stuart monarchy would be restored and the bodies of her family would be buried in Westminster Abbey:

Edinburgh, 21 May 1718
… she sickened upon sunday night 1 May new stile it was a continowed feaver with redoublement on thursday it turned worse, on frayday night still higher and appeared mortall, so about midnight she received the rites of the church sent her blessing to her son, and seemed much concerned for him as her only care, desired he might be informed of her last dying words to persevere in his profession what ever should happen, and continowing sensible till the last expired saturday the 7 betwixt 7 and 8 in the morning. Her testament being opened she ordered a part of her bowells to the monastry of Chaliot [Chaillot] and her body to be depositat there til on the restoration it should be transported with her husbands and daughters to Westminster…

The desolation amongst the followers of her son is inexpressible…

"*The desolation amongst the followers of her son is inexpressible*"

In her last years Mary Beatrice had sought refuge from the stresses of exile at the Convent of the Visitations at Chaillot near Paris, where she had found some solace.

Life in Exile
1716 - 1727

"Adieu for evermore... Never to meet again"

(Robert Burns)

Returning to Lady Winifred Nithsdale's dramatic story:

... everybody judged it prudent for me to leave the kingdom; for so long as the hatred of the king subsisted I could not be safe, and as it was not probable that I could escape falling into his hands, I accordingly went.

She was also desperate to be reunited with her husband in France.

But first Winifred, now in early pregnancy, had to return to Scotland to wind up affairs at Terregles. With the aid of the gardener who dug a deep hole in a secluded area of the garden, she buried a box of the family's legal writs and papers. (William's earldom and the Nithsdale estate had recently been forfeited as punishment for his role in the '15). She also had to go across to Traquair to collect her daughter before heading off on her long journey to London and onwards to Dover for the Channel crossing.

Terregles House
Dumfriesshire

The story is taken up by Mrs Evans, Winifred's attendant (under the 'nom de guerre' Mrs Powell), in a letter to Mary at Traquair. It was written at Sluce [Sluis], a Dutch seaport close to Bruges, on 28 June 1716:

My Lady Commands me to give your Ladyship an account that she is arrived at this place I Can't say she is come safe in health haveing Miscarried. The Stress of vomiting I Beleive Haveing been ye occasion of it, She Being very ------- when She Left London, we set off on Thursday 12 at night, and Came to this place on Sunday 3 in ye afternoon, dureing which Time She Had

Life in Exile

> "I was forc'd To Trust ye Captain of ye Ship with who she was att Last; and Indeed he has acted most Civilly"

a Continuall vomiting, I have been in many Dangerous Illness with her But Never like This... being so many passengers of both Sexes and we had no place to our selves goeing as Ordinary people, She Had a Bed Indeed but There was 7 more in ye Cabinne Besides us, I was forc'd To Trust ye Captain of ye Ship with who she was att Last; and Indeed he has acted most Civilly, we shall stay here Till she is past Danger, for we Cant goe To Bruges from hence by water but wagons or Coach, and that Jolting woud quite Ruine her yet...

Recovering sufficiently to make the journey to Bruges, Winifred was nursed back to health by her sister, Lucy, Mother Prioress at the English Convent there, before being reunited with William at Lille. Feeling very uneasy about their situation, he wrote to Mary at Traquair in a tone of exasperation:

Deare Sister
Had not my wives illnes occasioned in great parte by her travelling sooner then her strength permited, hindered me from writing, I should not have been so long without doing it, I am too sencible of my obligations to you and your Lord not to acknowlege them if I am not in a capasity of doing mor... we are hear in very dear place, but my sircumstances for reasons you may guess, permits me not to live in Spanish Flanders, I long to know what my wife will be permited to doe, that we may remove but as yett we know not...

William, Earl of Nithsdale, to his sister, Mary
Lille, 16 October 1716

Life in Exile

After leaving Paris William had joined the entourage of King James VIII at Avignon, but he had returned north to await Winifred's arrival from England. They parted company again when she persuaded him to rejoin James who had now left with his close followers for Italy. Winifred and her daughter took up residence in La Fleche in the Loire Valley where her son, William, was studying at the Jesuit College. They received a very welcome visit from Winifred's nephew from Traquair, Charles, Lord Linton, shortly after he set off from Paris on his Grand Tour of Europe.

By 1719 the exiled Stuart court was settled in the Muti Palace in Rome which had been offered to them as a permanent base by Pope Clement XI. He had just heard of James's engagement to Princess Maria Clementina Sobieska, youngest daughter of the King of Poland.

Muti Palace, Rome

William and Winifred were finally reunited in Rome (where they would spend the rest of their lives), but Winifred often complained bitterly to her sister-in-law about them not being welcomed by James into his inner circle.

However, there were occasions when she could not contain her excitement:

This Dearest Sister is barely to acquaint you that yesternight arrived here our young Mistress. I & my companion went out a post to meet her, & indeed she is one of ye Charmingest, obliging, & well brede young Ladys that ever was seen; our master cannot but be extreamly happy in her, & all those who has ye Good fortune to have any dependance on her, to add to it she is very pretty, has Good eyes, a fine skine, well shap't for her heath [height?], but is not tall, but may be so as yet, for she is but 17; & looks even younger...

"one of ye Charmingest, obliging, & well brede young Ladys that ever was seen"

Life in Exile

Princess Maria
Clementina Sobieska
(Queen Clementina)

Before long Winifred was eager to relay the news of the royal pregnancy but her delight was tainted by the fact that she had not been one of the first to hear about it:

Tho I have but a moment of time Deare Sister yet I would rather write but a line than difer a post to lett you know that our young Mrs [Mistress] is with quick Child, God almighty be praysed… which I am sure noe body does more rejoice at them my selfe, tho I must tell you at the same time that I was never was acquainted with it, till it was publickly told, & that Mrs Hay had felt it stire, who is one as you know that has never had any Children…

… all these behaviours join'd to what I have already acquainted you with, makes me supose that when it is born I shall have as litle to doe then as I have now…

She continued in some distress:

… we cannot live & put our selves in decent clothes with what is allow'd us, so must goe to some cheaper place, where I may live quietly, & out of ye dayly slights & mortifications which I daily suffer… I beg you that as soon as this comes to your hands, you will lett me know yours & your husbands opinion, for it is by my Husbands orders that I write this to you, so beg you will not difer your answer…

"ye dayly slights & mortifications which I daily suffer"

Early in 1721, the birth of Prince Charles Edward Stuart was dutifully reported to Traquair, and this was followed a few weeks later by another letter from Winifred in which, after speaking about the "*fine child*", she informed Mary that the crisis regarding their immediate future had been resolved. She and her husband would remain in the Muti Palace for the time being in the hope that their status in James's court would improve.

Life in Exile

Winifred's news from the Stuart Court

17 May 1719

This Dearest Sister is barely to acquaint you that yesternight arrived here our young Mistress, I & my companion went out a post to meet her, & indeed she is one of ye Charmingest, obliging, & well brede young ladys, yt ever was seen; our master cannot but be extreamly happy in her, & all those who has ye good fortune to have any dependance on her, to add to it she is very prety, has good eyes, a fine shince, well shap't for her...

9 March 1720

...& put our selves in decent cloths with wt is alow'd us, I must goe to some cheapper place, where I may live quietly, & out of ye dayly slights, & mortifications wch I daily suffer; we have taken the resolution neither to see, here, nor understand till ye time is over; I beg you yt as soon as this comes to your hands, you will lett me know yours & your husbands opinion, for it is by ... husbands orders yt I write this to you, so beg you...

4 February 1721

...in my last dearie Sister I had only time to give you the comfortable newse yt our Mrs was safly brought to bed of a son, & not to answer your letter of ye ... of november, if I had it, as I ought to have had but it came but a post agoe, & I was willing to stay one ... might at ye same time I answer'd it, send ye ... the assurance of her being happily recover'd & having been abroad, her Son is also very prety, & a fine child God bless him, & ye father, as you may be sure, not a little fond of him, I am glad you thinke my reasons solid for my not quitting this place, if I did not thinke it was for ye good of my family; I must confess, a private ... would have been more suitables to my inclinations, but we live for others in this world, & not our selves, & duty must still be preferr'd, & wt ever ye event may be, I will endeavour to omit noe part of it ... leave ye rest to God...

Dearest Sister
Your most ... & very humble servant
W. Johnston

Life in Exile

In my last Deare Sister I had only time to give you the comfortable newse that our Mrs [Mistress] was safely brought to bed of a Son... send you the assurance of her being happily recover'd, & having been abroad, her Son is also very well, & a fine child, God bless him, & ye father, as you may be sure, not a litle found [fond] of him; I am glad you thinke my reasons solid for my not quiting this place, if I did not thinke it was for ye good of my family; I must confess a privater would have been more suitable to my inclinations; but we live for others in this world, & not our selves, & duty Must still be prefer'd...

The young
Prince Charles Edward Stuart
1720 - 1788

Clementina gave birth to her second child, *"another brave boy"*, Prince Henry Benedict Stuart, on 6 March 1725, but by this time all was not well in the royal household. Amid rows, intrigue and accusations, Clementina left the Muti Palace to take up residence in the Convent of St. Cecilia. Some time later James moved his young sons temporarily to Bologna where they could lead a more private life. This worked out very well for Winifred and William although it resulted in their separation for a time. Winifred, whose status had indeed improved, was given unofficial care of the two princes, with particular responsibility for Charles Edward's religious education, and she accompanied them to Bologna. William remained in Rome to wait upon the queen.

The financial obligations of the Earl and Countess of Traquair to the Earl and Countess of Nithsdale ended in 1727 when King James VIII made this formal announcement:

Our will and pleasure is that you forthwith swear and admit Our Right Trusty and Right well beloved Winifred Countess of Nithsdale into the place and quality of governess of our dearly beloved son Henry Duke of York. To have and to hold the said place with all the offices salaries perquisites and advantages there unto belongs. Given at our court at Bologna this 4th day of July 1727. In the 26th year of our reign. Signed James R.

By this time William's position in the court was guaranteed too.

The 1745 Jacobite Rising
1745 - 1746

*"Come weel, come woe, we'll gather and go
And live or die wi Charlie"*

(Robert Burns)

The attempt by King James VIII to regain the throne of Great Britain for the exiled House of Stuart had ended in failure in 1715. His son, Prince Charles Edward Stuart, now took up the cause. In his manifesto of 16 May 1745 Charles declared he was executing the will of his father in asserting his undoubted right to the throne of his ancestors. This raised the spirits of loyal Jacobites, giving them renewed hope of a Stuart restoration.

*"God Bless the Prince of Wales
The true-born Prince of Wales...
Send him soon over
And kick out Hanover
And then we'll recover
Our old Libertie"*

The prince sailed from France, landing on the Scottish isle of Eriskay on 23 July 1745. Having gathered a considerable number of Highland clansmen as supporters along the way, he raised the Jacobite standard at Glenfinnan on 19 August. On 15 September Charles Edward's forces reached Edinburgh and the city quickly surrendered, with only the castle holding out against them.

A Traquair Jacobite 'Amen' glass ('Amen' being the final word of the toast to the 'Prince o'er the water')

ⳄⳂ

Christian Anstruther, wife of the Honourable John Stuart, viewed this dramatic turn of events with a degree of alarm.

The 1745 Jacobite Rising

The Honourable John Stuart
(6th Earl of Traquair
from 1764)
1699-1779

From her home in St. Andrews in Fife she wrote to her mother-in-law at Traquair, begging her to exert her influence over her son "*to keep him at home*" and not join "*the publick enterprize*":

... had I had the Honour of being with you; I am perswaded it wou'd have saved me many ane anxious moment, and many a sleepless night which I have suffered of late upon your son's account. As the publick enterprize bears no promising aspect I have hitherto been able to prevail with him not to join in it, but that has only given me the ease that a reprive would do to one under sentence of Death, every moment in terrour for what will be determined the nixt; I have represented to him that he can be of little consequence, as he has neither authority nor following, all he can do is to risk his Children's bread and a life so precious to me without being able to do any service. I therefore beg of your Ladyship (if ever mine or my Children's happiness was Dear to you) to join your Authority with my Prayers to keep him at home...

Christian Anstruther
(6th Countess of Traquair
from 1764)
d. 1771

Things were moving rapidly. James VIII was proclaimed King of Scotland with Charles as Prince Regent the day after Christian wrote of her anguish. And only three days later the Jacobite forces celebrated a resounding victory over the British Army under Sir John Cope at the Battle of Prestonpans just outside Edinburgh.

Having failed to take Edinburgh Castle, Prince Charles Edward set up court at the Palace of Holyroodhouse. He made excursions into the Scottish Borders to garner support for his cause, visiting Traquair where he received a warm welcome from Charles Stuart, 5th Earl of Traquair. On the prince's departure Charles locked the recently-erected Bear Gates at the head of the avenue, vowing that they would remain locked until the Stuart monarchy was restored.

After leaving Edinburgh early in November the Jacobite army, now made up of more than 5,000 foot soldiers and 500 cavalry,

The 1745 Jacobite Rising

headed into England, their goal being to reach London and remove the Hanoverian king, George II.

Later in the month Mary, now Dowager Countess of Traquair (her husband, the 4th Earl, having died in 1741), received this letter from William Drummond, 4th Viscount Strathallan, indicating that she had knowledge of the exact whereabouts of the Jacobite forces:

I am sure it will be agreeable to your La[dyshi]p to know by this that Lord John Drummond landed at Montross [Montrose] the 25th with a number of French. His Lo[rdshi]p expects more to Land dayly. I beg your La[dyshi]p will direct the bearer the safest way he can come at the Princes Army he haveing a Letter to deliver to the Secretary.

At the end of the year there was confusion and anxiety over in south-west Scotland. Mary's daughter, Catherine, married to her cousin, William Maxwell, son of William and Winifred, 5th Earl and Countess of Nithsdale, reported to her mother that the prince's army had suddenly appeared in Dumfriesshire, its steady advance on London having been reversed:

I doubt not but your Ladyship would be much surprised to hear of ye good company we have lately had in this part of ye world and I'm sorry to say that neither our town nor countrie deserved so great an honour, your Ladyship need not be alarmed at their sudden return which will certainly afford various speculations but one thing I can assure your Ladyship of that all our friends are in top spirits and thank God in perfect health and still seems sure of ye grand affair coming soon to a happie conclusion...

Catherine went on to express her uneasiness at her own situation - alone at the Maxwell family home at Terregles in pro-Hanoverian Dumfriesshire, her husband having gone into hiding as a Jacobite sympathiser:

Viscount Strathallan to Countess
Dowager of Traquair
26 November 1745

Hope and apprehension

Lady Catherine Maxwell
to her mother
26 December 1745

The 1745 Jacobite Rising

"if your Ladyship will be so good as to accept of me back again to Traquair till ye madness in this countrie is a little abated"

The long experience I have had of your Ladyships goodness and as I know you are a most affectionat and tender hearted Mother I therefore presume to give you this trouble to acquaint you that I am at present but in a very dismall situation and I may say with truth in a melancholy condition ye particulars of which I cannot commit to paper. All I cane say is that I wish to God I were so happie as to be again with you and to be a little more plain I don't think myself quite safe in staying here, so if your Ladyship will be so good as to accept of me back again to Traquair till ye madness in this countrie is a little abated, it will be a great comfort to me... and will take it as a singular favour if your Ladyship will allow Mr MacIver to come here ye beginning of ye next week and if he cane get a good horse either to hire or borrow for ridding double I shall be extreamlly obliged to him for my chaise and horses are all gone just now, and besides I would choose to travel incognito...

I beg with ye greatest earnestness you'll send for me which will really be doing an act of charity for were I to stay much longer here just now I'm sure I would loose my health and I believe break my heart.

I hope your Ladyship will pardon this confused letter which pray burn...

Mary immediately arranged for her daughter to return home.

The white cockade - a Jacobite emblem

In September 1745 a few of the workers at Traquair, showing their support for the family they served, had done their duty by taking part in some local action. Wearing white cockades in their bonnets, William MacIver, the earl's factor, with Baine and White, the gardeners, had gone into nearby Peebles intent on disarming Government troops stationed in the town. Six months later the law caught up with them:

The 1745 Jacobite Rising

Precognition of witness, Robert Paterson, against McIver, Baine and White, March 1746

... compeared Robert Paterson Mason in Peebles who declares that in the month of September last upon Monday the 23d of the said month he being standing upon his own stair which is next to the smiddy of John Ker smith he saw William McIver one Baine and White all servants to the Earl of Traquair having all on White Cockades, atacked two of his Majesties Soldiers... and William McIver order'd White... to keep and detain the Soldiers prisoners until they were Call'd for The prince's army, as he Called them, being seeking them in all Arts...

Two local Presbyterian Kirk ministers were happy to supply MacIver, "*a peaceable and inofficious Man*", with an impeccable reference, blaming "*the late unhappy Rebellion*" for his acting completely out of character:

3 June 1746
We Mr Gilbert Hutchisone Minister of the Gospel at Innerleithen, and Mr Alexander Davidson, Minister of the Gospel at Traquair... declare that We have known, and have had Business with William MacIver, Factor to the Right honourable the Earl of Traquair, for Several Years backwards, one of us upwards of Twenty Years, and that during our Acquaintance with him, he has bore, in this Country, the Character of a peaceable and inofficious Man, and lived (so far as we could have Access to know) a sober, regular and inoffensive Life, before the Commencement of the late unhappy Rebellion...

The 1745 Jacobite Rising

The Kirk was incensed by "*the present unnatural Rebellion*" and its Presbytery of Peebles, by a strange coincidence, appointed 16 April 1746 "*to be observed as a Day of Fasting, Humiliation and Prayer... on account of the many crying sins and abominations that abound in the Land*" - little realising that this would be the very day that the Battle of Culloden would put paid to the hopes and dreams of the Jacobites for ever.

... unanimously appoint Wednesday the 16th instant to be observed as a Day of Fasting, Humiliation and Prayer... earnestly obtesting all Ranks to humble themselves before God on the account of their own sins and the many crying sins and abominations that abound in the Land, and fervently to implore the Divine Mercy through Jesus Christ for averting these heavy Judgments with which he has visited us... and to preserve our valuable Rights and Privileges as men and Christians against all Attempts made by a popish Pretender and his Adherents at home and abroad to deprive us of them, and to offer up our joint Prayers and Supplications to Almighty God, that He would be pleased to bless and long preserve our only rightful Sovereign King George, The Prince and Princess of Wales, the Duke of Cumberland and all the Royal Family, and Direct His Majesties Councils at this critical Juncture, give Success to his Arms by Sea and Land, suppress the present unnatural Rebellion, and restore the publick Peace and Tranquillity...

"give Success to [King George's] Arms by Sea and Land, suppress the present unnatural Rebellion, and restore the publick Peace and Tranquillity"

Survivors retreating from the battlefield at Culloden

The Aftermath of the '45
1746 - 1748

*"Now a' is done that men can do,
And a' is done in vain!"*

(Robert Burns)

Prince Charles Edward Stuart went on the run immediately after the Battle of Culloden, with Government forces in hot pursuit. The Duke of Cumberland ('Butcher Cumberland'), received *"certain Information of the Young Pretenders sculking in the long Island"*, the prince having been sighted in the Outer Hebrides. Back on the mainland, he evaded capture and sailed for France in September 1746.

&

The failure of the '45 saw Lady Catherine Maxwell leave Traquair where she had taken refuge with her widowed mother. On her safe arrival home at Terregles a month after Culloden Catherine reported that there was still some residual ill-feeling towards Jacobites in her part of the world:

... I got safe home on Thursday's evening, and, thank God, without the least accident; but had I come by Dumfries I am told there was a mob prepared for my reception; however, I disappointed them, and am still without dread or fear, my own person being the least of my concerns at present. I only wish from my heart all our worthy good friends were as safe and well.... oh, God give a happy end to these miserable troubles.

In this letter Catherine also told her mother:

My brother [5th Earl of Traquair] is, for certain, married some months ago. Sir John Douglas says she is a very pretty, agreeable lady, and she is longing much to be in Scotland...

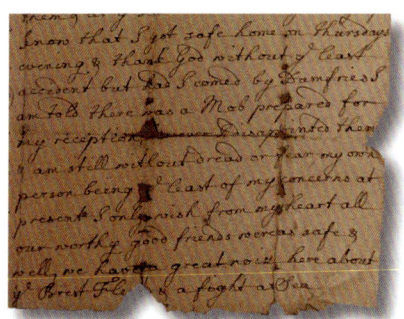

Lady Catherine Maxwell
to her mother
May 1746

The Aftermath of the '45

Theresa Conyers
5th Countess of Traquair
d. 1778

Charles Stuart
5th Earl of Traquair
1697-1764

After welcoming Prince Charles Edward to Traquair in the autumn of 1745, Charles had travelled down to Great Staughton in Huntingdonshire to marry Theresa, the daughter of Sir Baldwin Conyers, Bart. By July 1746 she had still not been able to visit Scotland. Writing to her mother-in-law, Mary, she said that she was distressed at not having been able to come to Traquair yet and that she felt *"too much for the sufferings of Scotland to dwell long upon so disagreeable a subject..."*. It was to be two years before Mary could meet her new daughter-in-law - her son, Charles, 5th Earl of Traquair, was arrested at Great Staughton and removed to the Tower of London.

So what was the 5th Earl's role in the '45? Two printed sources, "*Memorials of John Murray of Broughton, sometime Secretary to Prince Charles Edward, 1740 - 1747*" and Lord Elcho's "*A Short Account of the Affairs of Scotland in the years 1744, 1745, 1746*" include important details which do not appear in the Traquair family archives.

The earl's Examination, taken before the Lord Chancellor, the Duke of Newcastle, the Earl of Harrington and the Prime Minister, Henry Pelham, was held at Whitehall on 8 August.

Five days later, Murray of Broughton, the earl's neighbour in Peeblesshire (who was to turn King's evidence) was examined. Being asked when and by whom the first invitation had been made to 'the Pretender' to come to Scotland he replied to the best of his Memory, 'the first motion made in this affair was in 1740' but added that he had only been told about this in 1743 by the Earl of Traquair. It would appear that one Drummond (otherwise McGregor) had been sent to the Jacobite Court at Rome by the newly-formed Jacobite Association comprising the Earl of Traquair, Mr John Stuart, the earl's brother, Lord Lovat, the Duke of Perth, Lord John Drummond, uncle to the Duke of Perth, Sir James Campbell of Auchinbreck and Cameron of Locheil. Murray went on to say that the associators, at the same time, had sent a

The Aftermath of the '45

Memorial to Cardinal Fleury, King Louis XV's chief minister, in France to encourage him to send a body of troops into Scotland to support the Jacobite cause.

In spite of no charges having been brought against him, the Earl of Traquair was kept in strict confinement. On 13 October 1747, he wrote to the Duke of Newcastle about his fourteen-month ordeal, *"which can not fail to have affected my health, besides the great confusion which must attend my private affairs by a long absence... I most earnestly beg of your Grace's goodness to solicit his Majesty for my liberty, either by being dismiss'd or admitted to Bail"*. Soon after, he was granted *"permission to walk in the Tower, attended by an officer"*. After a further application to the Duke on 21 January 1748, the earl was released on bail. He was finally discharged in October of that year, without having stood trial (Being a prisoner had proved costly at seven guineas a week for a suite of three rooms for himself and his wife - not including the cost of wine, tea or warders' pay).

The aftermath of the 1745 Jacobite Rising spawned streams of invective, some directed specifically at the 5th Earl of Traquair. He was the target of a lengthy printed tirade viciously accusing him of betrayal of the Jacobite cause. It concluded:

Let the Jacobites rail against you never so bitterly, you know they are an unquiet restless Set of People, hard to be pleased, but let them blame themselves, not you, for the Confidence and Trust they foolishly reposed in you.

It would appear that the earl had been involved in planning for Prince Charles Edward's arrival in Scotland for several years, and that towards the end of 1744 he had been entrusted with a packet of letters to be delivered to the prince, now in Paris. The advice they contained was that the prince should not attempt a landing in Scotland without a considerable number of French troops and strong financial backing. It was still unclear how much of a

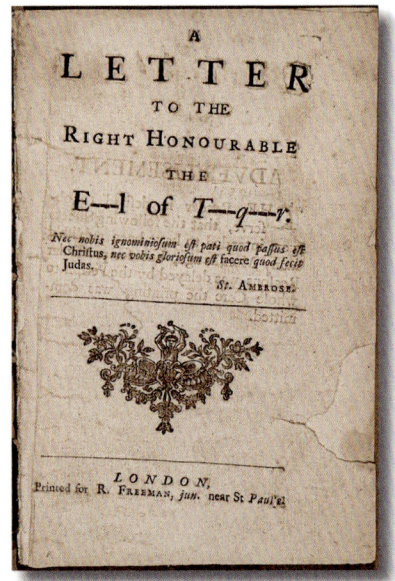

Pamphlet accusing 5th Earl of Traquair of being a traitor to the Jacobite cause (Anon.)

The Aftermath of the '45

following he could muster in the Highlands and how many English Jacobites could be relied upon to offer support. The earl was in London in January 1745 with the packet but, with the meagre monetary inducement on offer, failed to attract a messenger who would deliver it to the prince. John Murray claimed that the packet was returned to him four months later, that he had attempted to transmit it to the prince, but that it was too late because Prince Charles Edward was already on his way to Scotland.

On his return home towards the end of 1748 the Earl of Traquair must have realised that the gates, closed in the autumn of 1745 when spirits were high, would certainly not be reopened in his lifetime – if at all.

This Jacobite coded letter, found among the 5th Earl's papers, provides evidence of his involvement in the '45.

Last Vestiges of the Jacobite Dream 1795 - 1842

Largely as a result of the Stuart family of Traquair's longstanding loyalty to the Stuart monarchy, both before and after exile, its financial situation had become precarious. In 1784 Charles, 7th Earl of Traquair, embarked on a bold move which saw him uprooting his young family, heading for the Continent and, in the early 1790s, settling in Madrid where he hoped to establish a lucrative coalmining enterprise to restore his family's fortunes. In an endeavour to attract sponsorship he thought he would exploit his Jacobite credentials.

Charles sought a reference from Henry Benedict Stuart, younger brother of Prince Charles Edward and now Cardinal Duke of York, no doubt reminding him that as a child growing up in the Muti Palace in Rome his governess had been Charles's great-aunt, Lady Winifred Nithsdale. On his brother's death in 1788 Henry had claimed the throne of Great Britain, France and Ireland as King Henry IX – but there was no attempt at another Jacobite rising.

Charles received this reply from Henry, with the encouraging opening sentence, *"I have full cognisance of the merits and Prerogatives of your Family..."*:

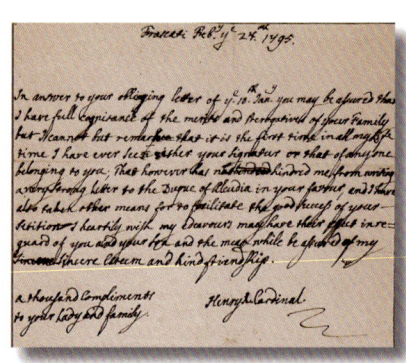

Henry Benedict Stuart, Cardinal York, to 7th Earl of Traquair; 'R' in his signature denotes 'Rex' (King)

Frascati Feb[ruar]y ye 24th 1795
In answer to your obliging letter of ye 10th Jan[uar]y you may be assured that I have full cognisance of the merits and Prerogatives of your Family but I cannot but remar~~quek~~ [sic] that it is the first time in all my Life time I have ever seen either your Signatur or that of any one belonging to you; That however has not hindred me from writing a very Strong Letter to the Duque

Last Vestiges of the Jacobite Dream

Bronze medal struck by Henry Benedict Stuart in 1788 when he proclaimed himself King Henry IX

of Alcudia in your favour, and I have also taken other means for to facilitate the good Success of your Petition – I heartily wish my e[n]deavours may have their effect in reguard of you and your Son and the mean while be assured of my Sincere esteem and kind friendship.

a thousand Compliments   Henry R. Cardinal
to your Lady and family

There was an ongoing correspondence between the two for some time, with Charles at pains to emphasise Henry's royal status, addressing him as *"your Royal Highness"* and ending his letters with his *"most profound Respect and Veneration for your Sacred Person"*. However, in spite of this Jacobite royal intercession and that of the Spanish royal family, his venture proved unsuccessful. The widowed 7th Earl returned to Traquair with his son and daughter in 1798 with his hopes and dreams shattered. His wife, Mary, had died in Madrid in 1796.

ଓ

The dawn of the 19th century witnessed a marked improvement in relations between the Stuarts of Traquair and the Georgian monarchy which, by now, was firmly established.

On 22 November 1806 King George III, under the Privy Seal of Scotland, granted Lady Lucy Stuart, the Jacobite 5th Earl's niece, a generous yearly pension of £200, and in 1822 the elderly and reclusive 7th Earl of Traquair received an invitation to the coronation ceremony of King George IV to be held in Edinburgh in August that year. This was being promoted by Sir Walter Scott and, imbued with his romantic vision of Scotland's past, promised to be a lavish spectacle. Lady Louisa Stuart, the earl's daughter, exhorted him to attend. She wrote:

King George IV during his coronation visit to Edinburgh in 1822

...Edinburgh is going to be so gay as the King is to visit Scotland, I hope you will pay your respects to his Majesty, as being the only Catholick Peer, it would appear particular if you did not, I

am sorry that I shall not be with you to inspect your Toillete as the wig you had at Terregles was rather shabby. I hope you will be able to get a good one made in Edinburgh... ask for life hair (which is softer than any other) that they may not give you the hair of a hanged man...

Lady Louisa Stuart to her father, 7th Earl of Traquair 12 August 1822

Since 1801 Lady Louisa had been living with her aunt in Surrey and was familiar with Georgian London society. However, both she and her brother Charles, Lord Linton, treasured their family's Jacobite past.

Charles wrote to his cousin Frances Jerningham, Lady Stafford, in February 1823:

...Tartans have been for some time past quite the fashion in Scotland among the Ladies and I think they look very handsome. The one I have sent you is the Stuart tartan, for as you are nearly related to a branch of that family, you ought to wear the tartan of no other clan.

The wearing of tartan had been banned under the Highland Dress Proscription Act rushed through Parliament following the Battle of Culloden. It had been regarded in London as intrinsically linked to the powerful clan system perceived to be largely responsible for the unrest. The Act had been repealed in 1782 by which time Jacobitism was no longer deemed to be a threat to the British Establishment.

Last Vestiges of the Jacobite Dream

Charles's fervour for all things Jacobite was intense. He continued:

I have sent Hog's Jacobite relicks in two volumes containing all the Jacobite songs that have been published, with the addition of some curious notes concerning them. You must learn these songs all by heart, sing one of them every morning when you rise, another before dinner and put the book under your pillow that you may dream of what you have sung during the course of day, till such time as you have fairly got the better of God save the King...

Charles, Lord Linton, to his English cousin, Frances, Lady Stafford February 1823

Two decades later, now 8th Earl of Traquair, he was buying outfits from a supplier of clothing and items with strong Jacobite associations, and dressing like a typical Highland laird. On 13 August 1842 he purchased from Meyer & Mortimer, trading as Royal Clan Tartan Warehouse, George Street, Edinburgh, a pair of chased silver shoe buckles with patent springs for £2 15s, a black velvet Highland Bonnet with band cockade & Silver thistle for £2 2s and 3 fine Eagles feathers for 7s 6d.

James Hogg's *'Jacobite Relics'*

Meyer & Mortimer's billhead proudly announced:

...having been appointed by the Highland Society of London to collect all the Clan Tartans of Scotland beg to inform the Public that they have a greater variety of Tartans than ever kept by any House... Have also on hand every Appointment requisite for the Highland costume, consisting of Broad Swords, Dirks, Pistols, Powder Horns, Purses, etc. etc. etc.

The outfit of a Jacobite Highlander had become fashionable, and the 8th and last Earl of Traquair had succumbed to its allure - no doubt wistfully contemplating the Jacobite past of his forebears.

"Wi' highland bonnets on their heads And claymores bright and clear
They cam' to fight for Scotland's right And for the Chevalier"
(James Hogg and Carolina, Lady Nairne)

ACKNOWLEDGEMENTS

We would like to thank John Nicholls MBE for allowing us to photograph and include images of the Nithsdale Escape cigarette card (p.28) and the Cardinal York medal (p.53); Harris Museum & Art Gallery, Preston, for the image of the painting of the Jacobite Surrender at Preston, 1715 (p.21), and Brian Vaughan from Traquair for the drawing of the Muti Palace, Rome (p.38).

We are also very grateful to John Fox for design and desktop publishing.

ଓଃ

Extracts from Minutes of the Presbytery of Peebles (pp.18 & 47) - Ref. NRS CH2/295
Digital images can be viewed in the Historical Searchroom in the National Records of Scotland, HM General Register House, Edinburgh. The original volumes are held by the Scottish Borders Archive, Heritage Hub, Hawick.

Front cover image: 'Prince Charles Edward Stuart leaving Traquair' by Tom Scott

© Traquair House Publishing 2017
All rights reserved. No part of this publication may be reproduced, stored in a retrieval system or transmitted in any form or by any means, electronic, mechanical, photocopying or otherwise, without the permission in writing of the publisher.

ISBN 978-1-9997559-0-4